MYSTERIES & MARVELS
OF
PLANT
LIFE

Barbara Cork

Consultant Simon Mayo

Designed by Anne Sharples

Illustrated by Ian Jackson
Kevin Dean, Sarah De Ath (Linden Artists)
Rob McCaig, Cynthia Pow, David Quinn
and Nigel Frey

Cartoons by John Shackell

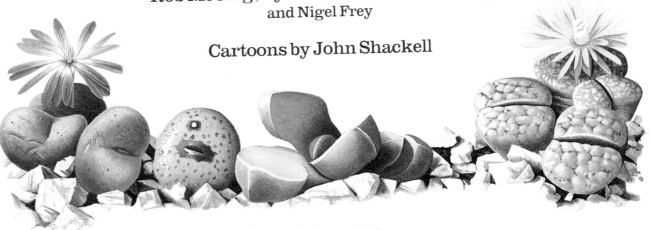

First published in 1983
by Usborne Publishing Ltd, 83-85 Saffron Hill,
London EC1N 8RT,
©1989, 1983 by Usborne Publishing Ltd.

The name Usborne and the device are Trade Marks
of Usborne Publishing Ltd.

Printed in Great Britain

Contents

Tank plants, ferns and mosses on a jungle branch.

Orchids

Amethyst Deceiver

Jack-in-the-Pulpit

Dragon Tree

Barrel Cactus

Seeds of the
Sterculia Tree

Flying Duck
Orchid

Orchids

Earth
Star

About this book

This book is a fascinating introduction to the amazing diversity of plant life, which ranges from giant Redwood Trees to tiny water plants no bigger than a full stop. Concentrating on the unusual, the extraordinary and the unexplained, it provides a stimulating starting point for the study of many aspects of plant life such as feeding habits, pollination, partnerships with insects and ways of surviving heat, drought and gale-force winds.

It looks at how some plants trap animals to eat and how others use deadly poisons and unusual tricks and disguises, such as laying "eggs" or looking like stones, to protect themselves from insects and grazing animals. It describes the way many flowers use animal messengers to carry their pollen and also rely on animals, the wind or ocean currents to disperse their seeds. It explains why an orchid makes bees drunk and some cucumbers explode.

This book will lead to an understanding of the many links plants have with animals and the environment around them but points out that there is still a great deal to be discovered about plants and the way they live.

Flowers of a
Ginger plant

Kangaroo
Paw

Honeyeater

TRUE or FALSE?

Look out for these questions and try to guess if they are true or false. The answers are on p. 32.

Climbers, stranglers...

Some jungle plants climb all over the jungle trees or perch on their branches. This helps them to escape from the dark, wet jungle floor and live nearer to the sunlight, which streams down on the roof of the jungle. They have special roots, stems and leaves to catch, carry and store water and nutrients.

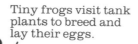

Tiny frogs visit tank plants to breed and lay their eggs.

▲ Swimming pool plants

Tank plants have a watertight cup of leaves, which collects a pool of rainwater, leaf litter and animal droppings. Special scales on the leaves take up water and nutrients from their private pool. Tadpoles, tiny insects and even a plant that eats insects may live in these tree-top pools.

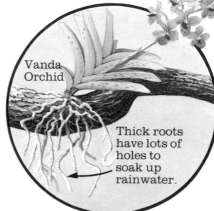

Vanda Orchid

Thick roots have lots of holes to soak up rainwater.

The strangler strikes again

1. A Strangler Fig grows from a seed that a bird or bat drops high up on a tree branch. The seed soon sprouts roots and leaves.

2. The roots eventually reach the ground and start to take up water and nutrients from the soil. The fig then begins to grow more rapidly.

3. The fig competes with the tree for light, water and nutrients. The tree may lose the battle and die, rotting away inside a living coffin.

▲ Orchid water tricks

About half the orchids in the world grow on other plants. They usually have thick leaves with a waxy surface, which helps to stop water escaping. Some of them have swollen stems to store water.

...thieves and murderers

Most plants use sunlight to make their own food from carbon dioxide (a gas in the air) and water. But some plants do not have the special green substance they need to capture the sun's energy. They steal their food from other plants instead and may eventually kill them.

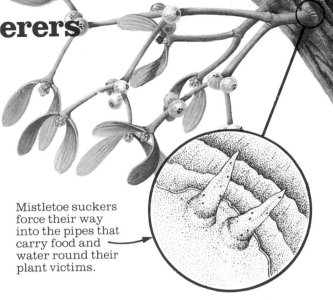

Mistletoe suckers force their way into the pipes that carry food and water round their plant victims.

A plant robber

The strange Broomrape plant has no green leaves so it cannot make its own food. It has to break into the roots of other plants and steal their food. But it can live only on broom and gorse plants and its seeds will die if they cannot find one of these plants to grow on.

broom

▲ Mistletoe – the vampire plant

Mistletoes have green leaves so they can make their own food but they also steal some food and water from the plant they grow on. Sometimes they kill the plants they feed from. There are even some mistletoes that grow on other mistletoes.

◀ Ropes to the jungle roof

The living "ropes" that Tarzan used to swing on are the woody stems of climbing plants called lianas. Special cells in their stems carry water up from the roots to the leaves, which grow in the sun above the giant jungle trees. In some lianas, water flows as fast as 1-2½ metres a minute.

Flower bud growing out of roots of a liana

The Rafflesia flower smells of rotting meat.

A plant without a body

This is the largest flower in the world. It is the only part of the Rafflesia plant that appears above ground. The rest of the plant is a network of threads that lives inside the roots of a liana. The plant steals all its food from the liana so it does not need a body with green leaves to make its own food.

TRUE or FALSE?

Lianas grow as tall as the Eiffel Tower and are strong enough to take the weight of an elephant.

Plant battlegames

Plants are in constant danger of attack from the animals that try to eat them. They use disguises, tricks, poisons and deadly weapons to battle for their lives.

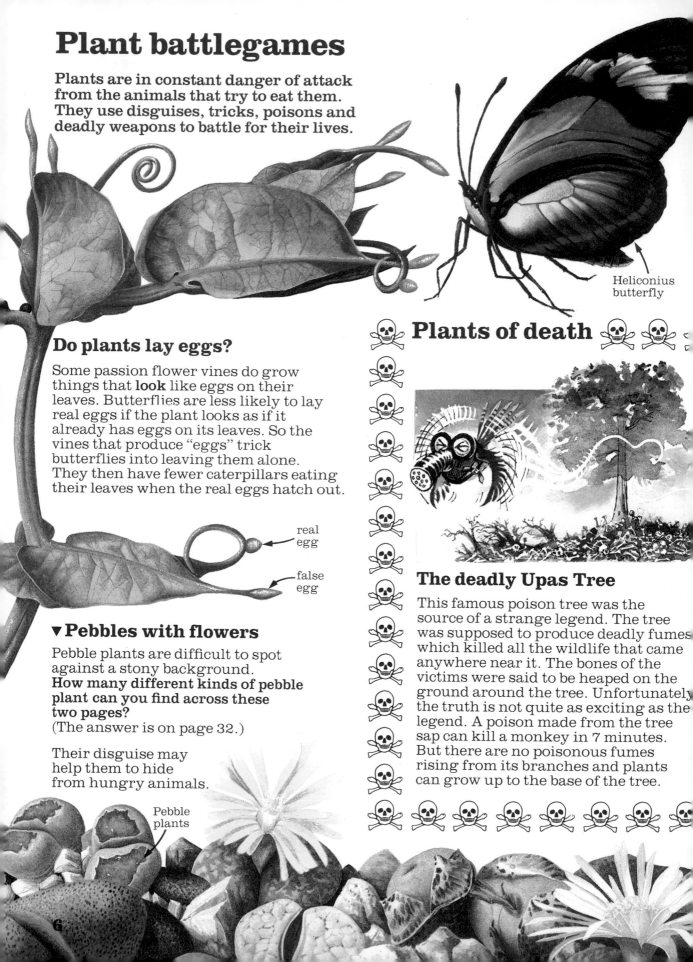

Heliconius butterfly

Do plants lay eggs?

Some passion flower vines do grow things that **look** like eggs on their leaves. Butterflies are less likely to lay real eggs if the plant looks as if it already has eggs on its leaves. So the vines that produce "eggs" trick butterflies into leaving them alone. They then have fewer caterpillars eating their leaves when the real eggs hatch out.

real egg

false egg

▼ Pebbles with flowers

Pebble plants are difficult to spot against a stony background.
How many different kinds of pebble plant can you find across these two pages?
(The answer is on page 32.)

Their disguise may help them to hide from hungry animals.

Pebble plants

Plants of death

The deadly Upas Tree

This famous poison tree was the source of a strange legend. The tree was supposed to produce deadly fumes which killed all the wildlife that came anywhere near it. The bones of the victims were said to be heaped on the ground around the tree. Unfortunately the truth is not quite as exciting as the legend. A poison made from the tree sap can kill a monkey in 7 minutes. But there are no poisonous fumes rising from its branches and plants can grow up to the base of the tree.

Savage spines

Many plants, especially cacti, are covered in very sharp spines, which helps to protect them from grazing animals. Some cacti have spines up to 15 centimetres long. Cactus spines have such perfect points that people have managed to play records using a cactus spine as the needle.

TRUE or FALSE?

Green potatoes can poison children.

Barrel Cactus

← The sharp spines are the leaves of the cactus.

Many plants contain deadly poisons, which may help to prevent animals from eating them. Fungi are the most poisonous. Some plant poisons can be used to treat human illnesses if they are given to the patient in very small amounts.

WORLD'S MOST POISONOUS FUNGUS

Death Cap

Deadly Nightshade
All parts poisonous to people but birds and rabbits can eat it. Used to widen pupils in eye surgery.

Koochla Tree
Source of strychnine. Causes convulsions and agonizing death. Can act as antidote to lead poisoning.

Foxglove
Eating 2½-4 leaves can cause death from heart attack. But used to treat heart disorders.

Laburnum
All parts poisonous. Children may mistake the seeds for peas. Causes convulsions, coma and death.

▼ The collapsing plant

The leaves of *Mimosa pudica* plants can suddenly collapse in just a few seconds. This may shake off insects that are trying to eat their leaves. The sudden movements may also help the plants to duck out of sight of grazing animals. As the plants also collapse at night and in cold weather, there is not a simple explanation for their strange behaviour.

A pair of swollen leaves on a pebble plant.

The strange ant plants

Some remarkable plants have their own special ants living inside their leaves, stems or even their thorns. The plants and their ants seem to help each other to survive by living together.

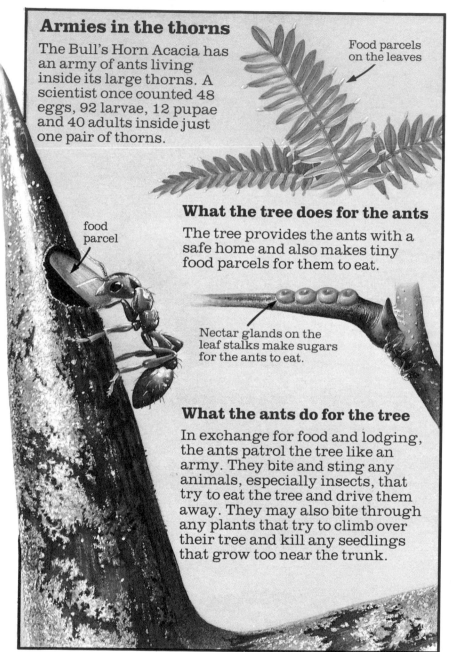

Armies in the thorns

The Bull's Horn Acacia has an army of ants living inside its large thorns. A scientist once counted 48 eggs, 92 larvae, 12 pupae and 40 adults inside just one pair of thorns.

Food parcels on the leaves

food parcel

What the tree does for the ants

The tree provides the ants with a safe home and also makes tiny food parcels for them to eat.

Nectar glands on the leaf stalks make sugars for the ants to eat.

What the ants do for the tree

In exchange for food and lodging, the ants patrol the tree like an army. They bite and sting any animals, especially insects, that try to eat the tree and drive them away. They may also bite through any plants that try to climb over their tree and kill any seedlings that grow too near the trunk.

▼ Ants in the leaves

The Dischidia plant grows leaf pouches, which often have ants living in them.

Ants live in here

These pouches are too wet for the ants.

This is what a leaf pouch looks like inside. The roots of the plant grow inside its own leaves. The ants are sheltered and protected inside their unusual home. The rubbish that they leave in their nest is probably a source of food for the plant. The roots in the leaf can take up this food.

Ants in the stems ▶

The Hydnophytum plant has a weird swollen stem with an amazing network of tunnels inside. Some of the tunnels have rough walls and others have smooth walls. Ants often live in the tunnels with the smooth walls. They leave soil, insect remains and other rubbish in the tunnels with the rough walls. The plant probably takes up food from the ants' waste heap.

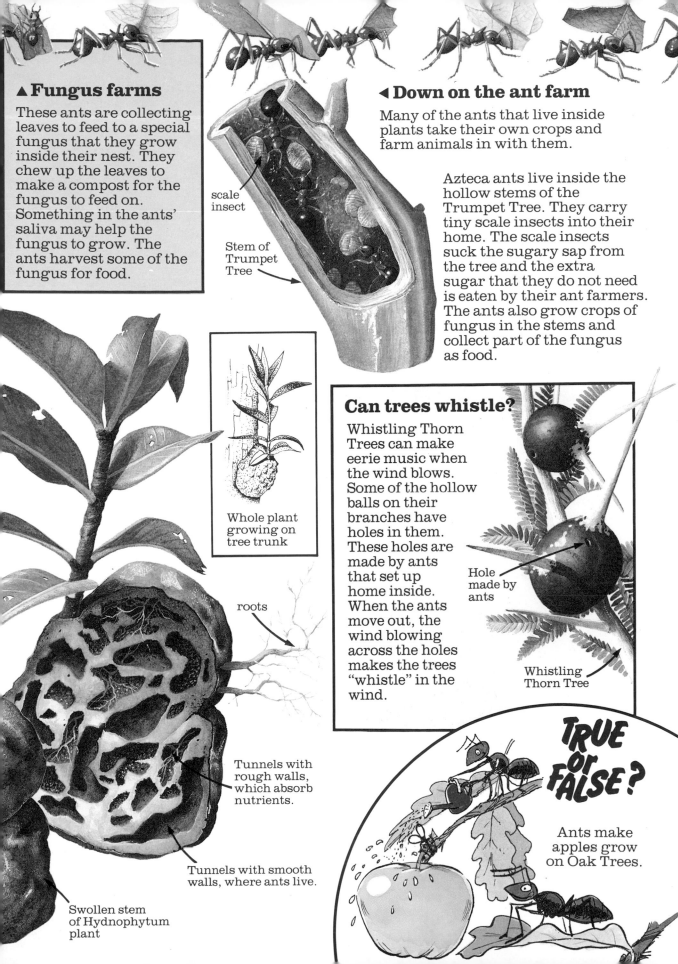

▲ Fungus farms

These ants are collecting leaves to feed to a special fungus that they grow inside their nest. They chew up the leaves to make a compost for the fungus to feed on. Something in the ants' saliva may help the fungus to grow. The ants harvest some of the fungus for food.

scale insect

Stem of Trumpet Tree

◄ Down on the ant farm

Many of the ants that live inside plants take their own crops and farm animals in with them.

Azteca ants live inside the hollow stems of the Trumpet Tree. They carry tiny scale insects into their home. The scale insects suck the sugary sap from the tree and the extra sugar that they do not need is eaten by their ant farmers. The ants also grow crops of fungus in the stems and collect part of the fungus as food.

Whole plant growing on tree trunk

Can trees whistle?

Whistling Thorn Trees can make eerie music when the wind blows. Some of the hollow balls on their branches have holes in them. These holes are made by ants that set up home inside. When the ants move out, the wind blowing across the holes makes the trees "whistle" in the wind.

Hole made by ants

Whistling Thorn Tree

roots

Tunnels with rough walls, which absorb nutrients.

Tunnels with smooth walls, where ants live.

Swollen stem of Hydnophytum plant

TRUE or FALSE?

Ants make apples grow on Oak Trees.

Plants that eat animals

Many plants are famous for their unusual habit of eating small animals, especially insects. But are there really killer plants that can eat elephants, dogs or even people?

Man-eating trees▶

There are many legends of man-eating trees, which curl their long, spiny branches round people and crush them to death. It is unlikely that these trees do exist but no one can really be sure.

Tricky trappers

Meat-eating plants lure their victims into deadly traps with colours, scents or the promise of food. The plants absorb extra nutrients from these strange meals, which helps them to survive in poor soils. Did you know that a type of geranium, some petunias, tobacco and even the **seeds** of Shepherd's Purse can kill and eat insects? There are probably more plants that eat animals waiting to be discovered.

Sundew plant

Sticky drops at end of tentacles

▼ Sticky sundews

Sundew plants catch insects on deadly tentacles that cover their leaves. Sticky drops at the end of the tentacles trap the insects. As they struggle to escape, the tentacles curl over and glue them firmly to the leaf so the plant can start its meal. The Portuguese Sundew takes about a day to eat a mosquito.

What they do with the bodies

Most meat-eating plants cover their victims in special juices, which turn the bodies into liquids. (You digest the food in your stomach in a similar way.) The plants soak up the liquid food through their "skin".

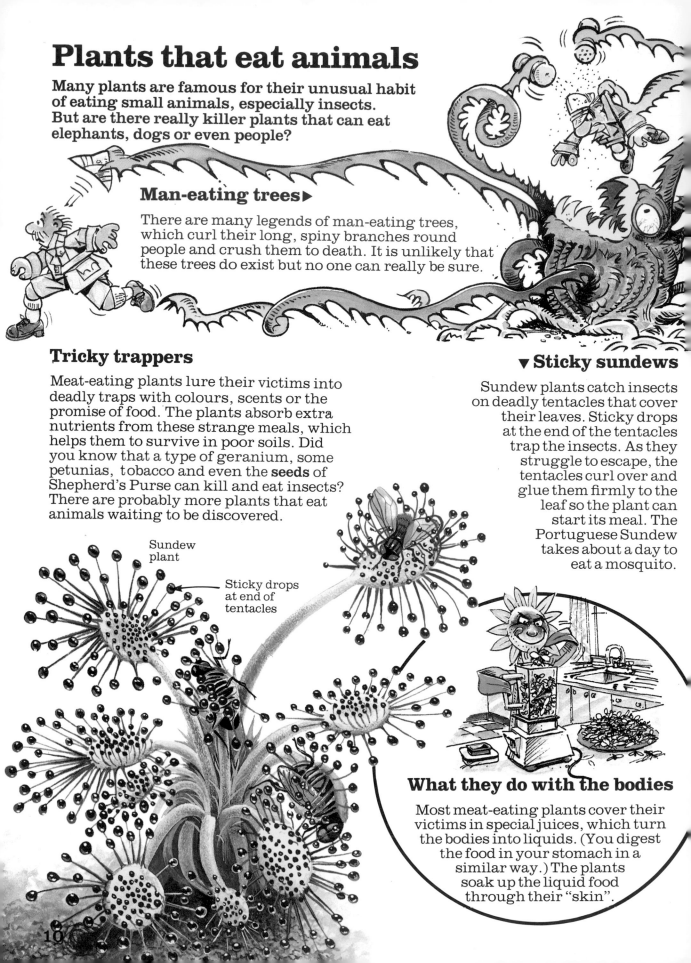

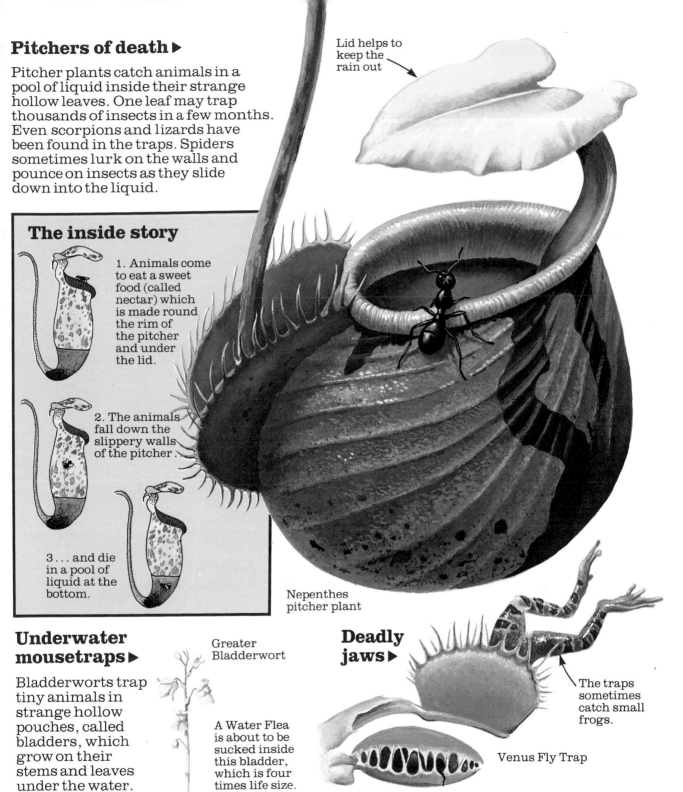

Pitchers of death ▶

Pitcher plants catch animals in a pool of liquid inside their strange hollow leaves. One leaf may trap thousands of insects in a few months. Even scorpions and lizards have been found in the traps. Spiders sometimes lurk on the walls and pounce on insects as they slide down into the liquid.

Lid helps to keep the rain out

The inside story

1. Animals come to eat a sweet food (called nectar) which is made round the rim of the pitcher and under the lid.

2. The animals fall down the slippery walls of the pitcher.

3 . . . and die in a pool of liquid at the bottom.

Nepenthes pitcher plant

Underwater mousetraps ▶

Greater Bladderwort

Bladderworts trap tiny animals in strange hollow pouches, called bladders, which grow on their stems and leaves under the water. A trapdoor keeps the bladder closed until an animal touches the hairs around the entrance. Some Bladderwort traps are only about the size of a full stop.

A Water Flea is about to be sucked inside this bladder, which is four times life size.

Deadly jaws ▶

The traps sometimes catch small frogs.

Venus Fly Trap

Venus Fly Traps have strange leaves that snap shut like a pair of jaws and trap their victims inside. The leafy jaws close only when something brushes against sensitive hairs on the surface of the leaf. Try growing a Venus Fly Trap yourself and see how many animals each leaf gobbles up.

Weird and wonderful flowers

Flowers are probably the most amazing structures in the plant world. Their wonderful shapes and colours are linked to their main purpose in life, which is to produce seeds. Some flowers need pollen from other flowers before their seeds can develop. They rely on the wind, water or animals to bring the pollen to them. Other flowers use their own pollen to produce seeds.

Marcgravia flower bud

Pouches full of sweet nectar

TRUE or FALSE?

Blue roses flower only in China.

Bird-of-paradise flower
Birds land here and pollen is brushed on to their feathers.

Pollen puzzle

These Birch Tree catkins are groups of male flowers, which produce the yellow dust called pollen.
How many pollen grains do you think each catkin produces?

One catkin can produce up to 5,500,000 pollen grains. Because there is so much pollen, at least some of it stands a chance of being blown by the wind to the female flowers so that seeds can develop.

The flower buds of the **Clove Tree** are dried and used as a spice in cooking.

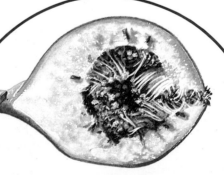

Fantastic fig flowers

The tiny flowers of figs are actually in the middle of the fig itself. Fig wasps carry pollen from the male to the female flowers.

◀ Curious clock flowers

Many flowers open and close at certain times of day. No one understands how these flower "clocks" work. They may help to protect the pollen from cold or rain, or they may make sure the flowers are open when animals are most likely to visit them. The famous botanist Carl Linnaeus planted a flower clock in his garden. He could tell the time by looking to see which flowers were open.

The rare **Lady's Slipper** is the largest European orchid with flowers up to 10 cm across.

male flowers

female flowers

The shoot lasts only a few days and smells of rotting meat.

Flowering shoot of *Amorphophallus prainii*

▼ Underground flowers

Two unusual Australian orchids live and flower below the surface of the soil. No one is sure how they manage to produce seeds. They may use their own pollen but if they do need pollen from the flowers on another plant, how does it reach them? This is still a mystery.

Trunks that sprout flowers

Many jungle trees have flowers that sprout straight out of their trunks and larger branches. This may make it easier for animals to find the flowers and feed from them. The trees rely on animals, such as bats, to pick up pollen while they are feeding and carry it to other trees.

13

Flower advertisements

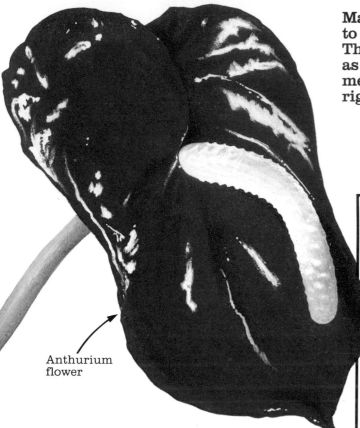

Anthurium flower

Many flowers rely on animal messengers to carry their pollen to other flowers. They use colour and scent signals as well as tricks and disguises to persuade the messengers to visit their flowers at the right time.

Secret signals for bees

Did you know that flowers attract bees with colours and markings you cannot see? For example, a Wild Cherry flower looks white to you but bees see it as blue-green. Bees can also see ultra-violet light, which is invisible to you. So they can see markings on this Evening Primrose flower that you cannot see.

Bees can see these markings on the flower.

The flower looks like this to us.

▲ Flowers in fancy dress

Brightly coloured structures around the flowers often attract animal messengers. The bright red hood on this Anthurium flower probably helps to attract insects to the yellow "tail" of tiny flowers.

Female impersonators ▶

Some extraordinary orchids attract male insects with flowers that look, smell and feel like females of their own species. This Mirror Orchid attracts a species of wasp. The male wasps appear earlier in the year than the females so the orchid flowers open when the males appear — before they have real female wasps to compete with.

furry "body"

folded "wings"

Smelly flowers ▶

Many flowers produce perfumes to attract animal pollen carriers. Sometimes these perfumes smell very unpleasant to us. This Stapelia flower reeks of decaying flesh. This smells like a tasty meal to flies that feed on rotting flesh so they are tricked into visiting the flower.

Stapelia flower

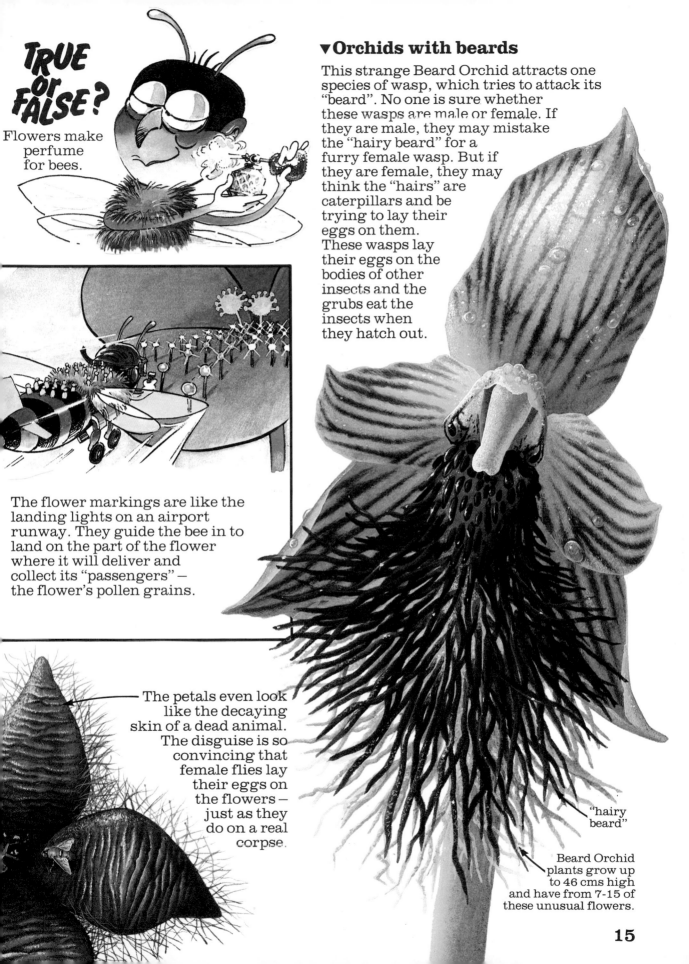

The flower markings are like the landing lights on an airport runway. They guide the bee in to land on the part of the flower where it will deliver and collect its "passengers" — the flower's pollen grains.

The petals even look like the decaying skin of a dead animal. The disguise is so convincing that female flies lay their eggs on the flowers — just as they do on a real corpse.

▼Orchids with beards

This strange Beard Orchid attracts one species of wasp, which tries to attack its "beard". No one is sure whether these wasps are male or female. If they are male, they may mistake the "hairy beard" for a furry female wasp. But if they are female, they may think the "hairs" are caterpillars and be trying to lay their eggs on them. These wasps lay their eggs on the bodies of other insects and the grubs eat the insects when they hatch out.

"hairy beard"

Beard Orchid plants grow up to 46 cms high and have from 7-15 of these unusual flowers.

Pollen take-aways

Once a plant has attracted an animal messenger to its flowers, it has to try and make sure the messenger delivers and collects some pollen. Many plants reward their messengers with a sweet food called nectar, or a place to lay their eggs. This means they are more likely to visit the flowers again.

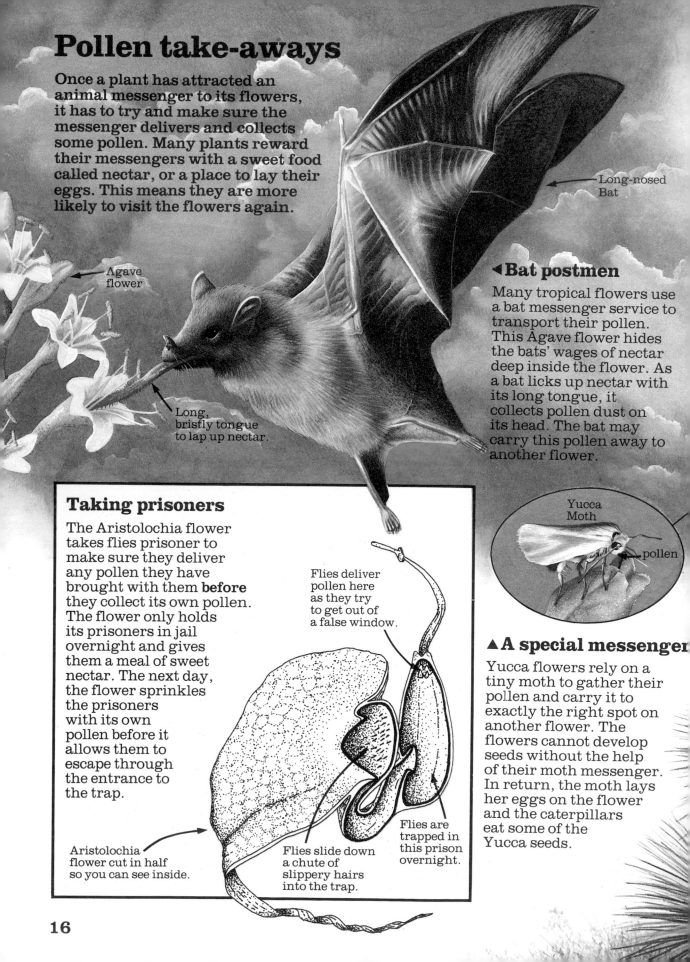

Long-nosed Bat

Agave flower

Long, bristly tongue to lap up nectar.

◀ Bat postmen

Many tropical flowers use a bat messenger service to transport their pollen. This Agave flower hides the bats' wages of nectar deep inside the flower. As a bat licks up nectar with its long tongue, it collects pollen dust on its head. The bat may carry this pollen away to another flower.

Yucca Moth

pollen

▲ A special messenger

Yucca flowers rely on a tiny moth to gather their pollen and carry it to exactly the right spot on another flower. The flowers cannot develop seeds without the help of their moth messenger. In return, the moth lays her eggs on the flower and the caterpillars eat some of the Yucca seeds.

Taking prisoners

The Aristolochia flower takes flies prisoner to make sure they deliver any pollen they have brought with them **before** they collect its own pollen. The flower only holds its prisoners in jail overnight and gives them a meal of sweet nectar. The next day, the flower sprinkles the prisoners with its own pollen before it allows them to escape through the entrance to the trap.

Flies deliver pollen here as they try to get out of a false window.

Aristolochia flower cut in half so you can see inside.

Flies slide down a chute of slippery hairs into the trap.

Flies are trapped in this prison overnight.

Nectar — the super fuel ▶

Hummingbirds need the high-energy nectar they sip from flowers to power their amazingly rapid flight. They can beat their wings as fast as 80 times per second and hover motionless in front of flowers. If a person used up energy at the same rate as a Hummingbird, they would have to eat 150 kilograms of hamburgers every day.

Penstemon flower

Hummingbird

Yucca plant

▼Bees get drunk on orchids

The amazing Bucket Orchid produces a special nectar that makes bees drunk enough to fall into a pool of water inside one of its petals. As a bee staggers up an escape tunnel, the flower's pollen sacs stick to its body.

TRUE or FALSE?

Orchids are used to make ice cream.

A false female ▶

This male Ichneumon Wasp thinks the Tongue Orchid is a female wasp. He glues the orchid's pollen sacs to himself as he tries to mate with the flower.

pollen sacs

Tongue Orchid

◀Bee transport

Milkweed flowers pack all their pollen into strange waxy bags. As bees sip nectar from the flowers, the bags may clip on to their legs and be carried off to another Milkweed flower.

Seed hitch-hikers

Seeds stand a better chance of growing into new plants if they do not have to compete with their parents for light, water and nutrients. They may travel away to a new area by hitching a ride on the wind, water currents, passing animals or sometimes even car tyres.

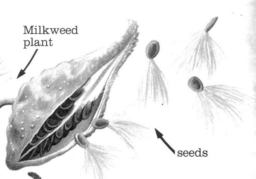

Milkweed plant

seeds

▲ Ocean travellers

Coconuts float away from their parent trees on the ocean currents. They may drift for several months and travel for up to 2,000 kilometres before reaching dry land. Special fibres around the seeds help the coconuts to float.

◄ Plant parachutes

Each Milkweed seed with its parachute of fluffy white fibres, can float on the wind for many kilometres. The fibres are so light that they have even been used to fill life jackets, which keep people afloat in water.

Exploding cucumbers

The Squirting Cucumber gets its name from its strange fruits. They burst open to shoot its seeds up to 8 metres away from the parent plant. The seeds zoom off like bullets from a gun and may travel as fast as a hundred kilometres per hour.

Wind witches ►

Are there really giant witches that chase people over the plains in Russia? These legends are probably based on the unusual behaviour of a plant that uproots itself and rolls along in the wind to scatter its seeds. If large numbers of these plants become hooked together, they may look like "wind witches".

Seed stowaways

Many seeds stow away on the bodies of furry animals. Burdock seeds have rows of hooks to grip the coat of a passing animal. They may be carried several kilometres before they are brushed off by the undergrowth. If they land on a suitable patch of soil, they have a good chance of growing into new plants.

Burdock seed

The Durian is a favourite food of the Orang-utan.

The smelly Durian ▲

The Durian fruit attracts many mammals with its strange smell. It may grow as large as a football and has custard-like flesh around the seed. When animals eat the fruits, the seeds pass through their bodies unharmed and come out in their droppings. This may be some distance from the parent tree.

Some seeds get about in the mud on animals' feet. Charles Darwin once grew 80 plants from the mud he scraped off a bird's foot.

◄ Seed kites

The seeds of the Chinese Lantern are blown away from their parent plant inside shining red kites. The kite on the left is one that did not get away. You can see the seed inside.

Paeonia obovata

▲ A colourful peony

The bright pink seeds of this peony seem to develop just to attract birds. They cannot grow into new plants. Birds eat all the seeds, which eventually pass out in their droppings. If the blue seeds land on a suitable patch of ground, they may grow into new plants.

TRUE or FALSE?

Mexican beans jump away from their parent plant.

19

Fantastic fungi

Fungi are very curious plants. They have a "body" of tiny branching threads, which can absorb food from living or dead plants or animals. Sometimes the threads weave together to make fruiting bodies, which often look like mushrooms but may be more unusual shapes, such as "ears". The fruiting bodies produce the spores of the fungus, which can grow into new plants. They often seem to pop up from the ground with almost magical speed.

◀ Fur coat fungi

The ermine coat worn by this beetle is the white threads of a mould fungus, which is feeding on its body. Some fungi even feed on people. Athlete's foot and ringworm are caused by fungi feeding on human skin.

Ear fungus

▲ Even trees have ears

This strange "ear" is the fruiting body of a fungus that feeds on dead wood. If fungi did not eat up dead material, the world would be a huge rubbish dump piled high with litter.

TRUE or FALSE?

Fungi are strong enough to grow through roads and pavements.

Truffle

◀ Strange partners and pigs

Truffles are the fruiting bodies of a fungus that grows only in a strange partnership with tree roots. The fungus takes food from the tree but makes some nutrients in the soil available to the tree in return. Truffles rely on animals to dig them up, eat them and spread the spores in their droppings. They attract animals by producing some of the smells the animals make themselves.

Animal trappers ▼

A few microscopic fungi have special traps to catch tiny animals. These range from sticky threads and fishing lines to nooses, which squeeze shut when eelworms try to wriggle through. Some fungus **spores** can follow the scent trail worms leave in the soil.

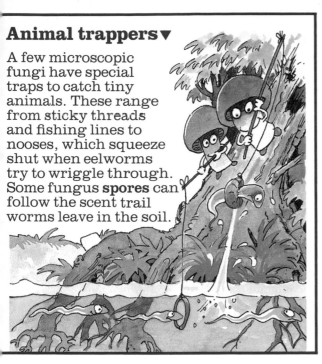

Do fungi make nests?

Some strange fungi grow fruiting bodies that look like birds' nests. They even have eggs inside. The "eggs" are, in fact, cases full of spores, which often jump out of the nest when rain drops splash inside. Some spore cases even have sticky tails, which help them to cling on to another plant before they reach the ground.

spore case

A stinking cage ▼

This strange Cage Fungus takes only a few hours to grow. The black slime inside the cage contains spores and gives out a foul smell. This attracts flies, which eat the slime and spread the spores in their droppings.

Flies feeding on slime

Puffball prizewinners

Puffballs release small clouds of minute spores, which are carried by the wind to new ground. An average-sized Giant Puffball 30 centimetres across can produce 7,000,000,000,000 spores. If all these spores grew into mature puffballs, they would stretch thousands of times round the earth.

Rich grass where fungi are releasing nutrients.

Grass may wither where fungi have used up nutrients.

▲ Fairy rings

People have blamed rings of toadstools on fairies, whirlwinds, haystacks, moles or underground smoke rings. But the strange rings are really formed by giant colonies of toadstools growing outwards year by year from a central point. Some rings may be 600 years old.

Marvellous mini-plants

Some of the smallest plants in the world can trace their ancestors back over 2,000,000,000 years. A few of them can survive in blocks of ice or nearly boiling water. Some even live on hairs.

Diatom spaceships

These weird structures, which look like pill boxes, sieves or even spaceships are all kinds of tiny plants called diatoms. They live in water and in the soil and are so small about 2,500 would fit along this line _____. You need a microscope to see their strange shapes.

The sloths' hidden secret ▶

Some minute plants, called algae, live in grooves on the hairs of sloths, which makes the hair look greenish. This helps sloths to blend into the leafy background of their jungle home so that they are safer from enemies. Sloths never clean their fur so the algae do not get washed off the hairs.

What makes snow red?

Mysterious patches of red snow sometimes appear on mountains. They are caused by vast numbers of tiny algae. Each plant is about as big as this full stop.

▼ Strange spore holders

Some mini-plants produce their spores in strange structures, which look like horns, matchsticks, Chinese pagodas or even jam tarts.

Stag's-horn Clubmoss
Yellow "horns" a few cms high hold the spores. Clubmosses 30 metres high lived 300,000,000 years ago.

Sphagnum Moss
The capsule fires its spores into the air like airgun pellets. The spores may land up to 2 metres away.

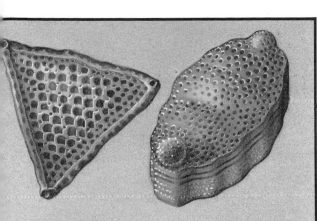

Diatoms are very simple plants consisting of one cell with a coat of silica round it. Each species of diatom has a different pattern of ridges, furrows and holes in its silica coat.

Plants that eat rocks ▶

The amazing coloured patterns on these rocks are actually tiny plants called lichens. The brilliant colours are lichen acids, which help to protect the plants from strong sunlight. The lichens also produce different acids, which eat into the rocks and make them crumble. Then they send out tiny "roots" to absorb minerals from the rocks. By breaking up the rocks in this way, the lichens slowly turn them into soil, where other plants can grow.

TRUE or FALSE?

Clubmosses are used to make fireworks.

alga

fungus

rock

◀ Living together

Lichens are two plants, an alga and a fungus, which live together in a strange partnership. The alga provides the fungus with food. In return, the fungus holds water for the alga and protects it from fierce winds and too much strong sunlight.

▼ The lichen mystery

These lichen fruiting bodies are made by the fungus partner in the lichen. The spores inside them cannot grow into a new lichen unless they find the right sort of alga to grow with. No one is sure how this happens.

Cup Lichen
Spores are produced round the rim of the cups.

Devil's Matches
Red tips of lichen produce spores.

Lecanora Lichen
Brown discs hold the spores.

Lunularia Liverwort
Special cups have small "buds" inside, which can form new plants. The "buds" splash out in raindrops.

Life at the top

High up on mountains, the strong sunlight, fierce winds, thin soils and freezing night-time temperatures make life very difficult for plants. Yet some amazing plants manage to survive there.

The white colour helps to reflect strong sun, which may harm the flower.

The flowering spike of the Silversword is about 2 metres high.

Silversword

Silverswords from Hawaii

The spectacular Silversword lives only on the tops of old volcanoes on two Hawaiian islands. Only about 7 centimetres of rain fall each year so the Silversword may take 20 years to store enough water for flowering. A few weeks later, the plant dies.

Furry flowers ▶

The European Edelweiss has a thick coat of hairs, which help to trap the warmth of the sun and stop water escaping from the plant.

Vegetable sheep

Some mountain plants grow close to the ground with their short stems packed tightly together to form strange cushions. This helps them to escape from the wind and they can also trap heat in the cushion. In some places, these cushions grow so big they have been mistaken for sheep.

Elfin woods ▶

Did you know that the trees on some mountains are so small you can walk over the top of them? Dwarf Willows grow in dense carpets only a few centimetres high. Their branches bend easily so they can twist and turn close to the ground. There they are out of reach of the fierce winds, which may be strong enough to blow a person over.

Plants with central heating

The tiny shoot of the Alpine Snowbell produces enough heat to melt a hole in the snow. It can then reach the surface to flower in early spring.

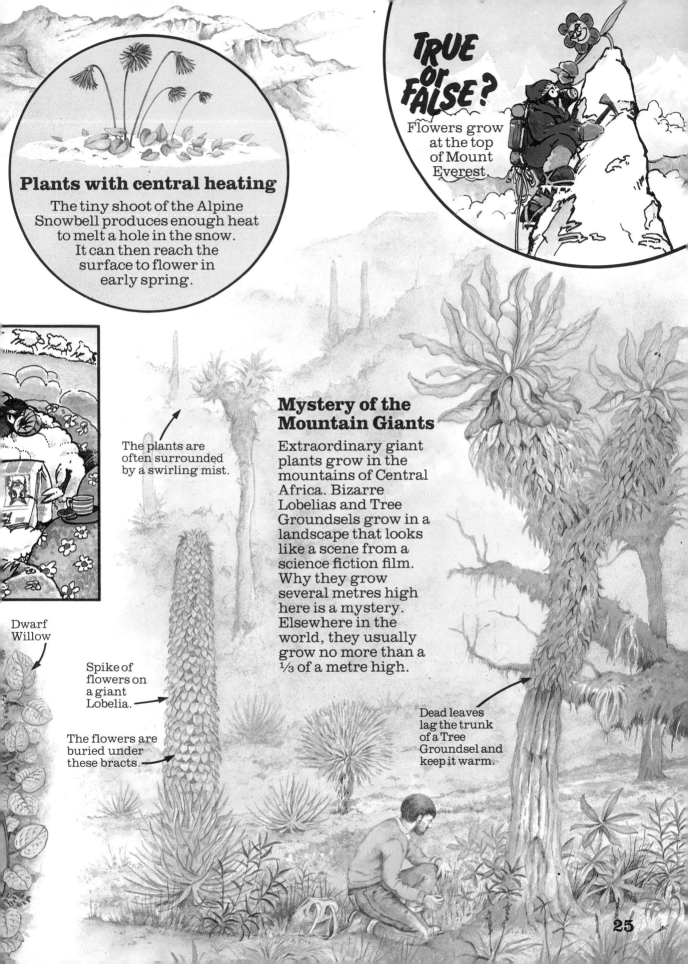

TRUE or FALSE?

Flowers grow at the top of Mount Everest.

The plants are often surrounded by a swirling mist.

Dwarf Willow

Spike of flowers on a giant Lobelia.

The flowers are buried under these bracts.

Mystery of the Mountain Giants

Extraordinary giant plants grow in the mountains of Central Africa. Bizarre Lobelias and Tree Groundsels grow in a landscape that looks like a scene from a science fiction film. Why they grow several metres high here is a mystery. Elsewhere in the world, they usually grow no more than a $\frac{1}{3}$ of a metre high.

Dead leaves lag the trunk of a Tree Groundsel and keep it warm.

Not a drop to drink

It takes a very special sort of plant to cope with the boiling hot days (up to 83°C), freezing nights and the dry soils of a desert. Desert plants have special features such as spines, vast root systems and deadly poisons to help them survive.

The **Gila Woodpecker** may nest in a Saguaro Cactus. It can be up to 30°C cooler inside.

▲Blooming magic

Many plants survive the dry season as seeds buried in the desert sands. As soon as there is enough rain, they suddenly sprout and produce flowers and seeds. The seed of one African plant (*Boerhavia repens*) takes only 8 to 10 days to grow into a mature plant, and produce seeds of its own.

▲The leaf trick

In the dry season, the Ocotillo plant sheds all its leaves so that it does not lose moisture through them. It grows a new set of leaves as soon as it rains.

Barrel Cactus spines have been used as fish hooks.

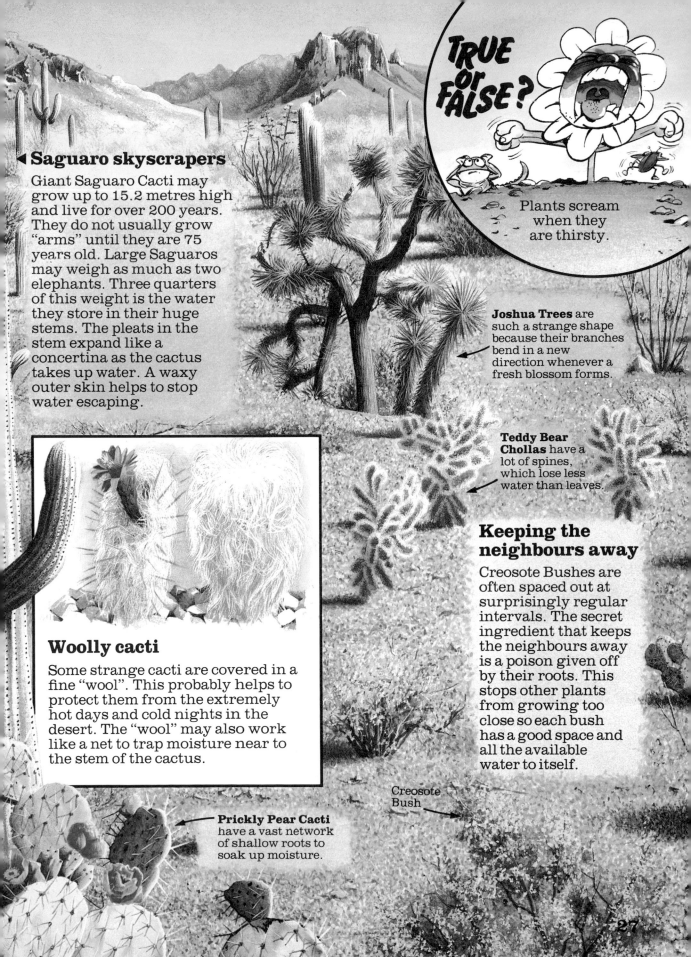

◄ Saguaro skyscrapers

Giant Saguaro Cacti may grow up to 15.2 metres high and live for over 200 years. They do not usually grow "arms" until they are 75 years old. Large Saguaros may weigh as much as two elephants. Three quarters of this weight is the water they store in their huge stems. The pleats in the stem expand like a concertina as the cactus takes up water. A waxy outer skin helps to stop water escaping.

TRUE or FALSE?

Plants scream when they are thirsty.

Joshua Trees are such a strange shape because their branches bend in a new direction whenever a fresh blossom forms.

Teddy Bear Chollas have a lot of spines, which lose less water than leaves.

Keeping the neighbours away

Creosote Bushes are often spaced out at surprisingly regular intervals. The secret ingredient that keeps the neighbours away is a poison given off by their roots. This stops other plants from growing too close so each bush has a good space and all the available water to itself.

Woolly cacti

Some strange cacti are covered in a fine "wool". This probably helps to protect them from the extremely hot days and cold nights in the desert. The "wool" may also work like a net to trap moisture near to the stem of the cactus.

Creosote Bush

Prickly Pear Cacti have a vast network of shallow roots to soak up moisture.

Plant mysteries

▼ Strange seed showers

Many people claim to have been pelted with thousands of seeds that suddenly fell down from somewhere high in the sky. Rice, wheat, barley and even hazelnuts have been reported in these strange showers. The cause is a mystery although people have blamed the showers on whirlwinds or strong winds high up in the atmosphere.

This fungus glows green but other species produce blue, white or yellow light.

The secret life of plants

Plants seem to respond to people, noises and other things around them in ways that no one really understands. But many people claim to have made startling new discoveries that could change the way we think about plants. Try testing some of these ideas on your own plants.

◄ Night lights

Many plants, especially fungi, produce an eerie light at night. Some fungi even produce enough light to read by. No one knows why they do this. Some scientists have suggested that the fungi use the light to attract the flies they need to scatter their spores. But why should some geraniums, marigolds and mosses glow in the dark?

People with "green fingers"

Why are some people especially good at growing plants? No one is really sure but plants seem to be able to respond to people praising them and wanting them to grow well. Some people produce chemicals in their sweat that may help plants to grow better.

Can plants read your mind?

Some people claim that a plant will react if you just **think** about burning one of its leaves. Other experiments seem to show that plants will grow badly or even die if people keep thinking nasty thoughts about them.

Do plants grow better to music?

Many people think they do. Some people even claim that Bach and classical Indian Sitar music is better for plants than rock music. Research has shown that crop plants grow better to the vibrations of an electric motor and loud noises can make seeds sprout more quickly.

Can plants remember?

Some people claim that a plant "remembered" the killer of a plant that was growing next to it and even picked out the guilty person from a group of people. Other experiments have shown that plants can "remember" injuries to their leaves.

▲The twisted tree mystery

The reason for the weird twisted trunk of this tree is a mystery. Some people think that a radioactive meteor may have caused the trunk to start growing in this strange way hundreds of years ago.

◄The mystery of the veiled lady

No one is sure why this tropical Stinkhorn Fungus has such a fantastic lacy veil. It may help to make the fungus more attractive to the flies that it needs to carry its spores away. The fungus grows as fast as 5mm a minute and some people believe it is magical.

How do bamboos count?

Some bamboos flower at very strange times. A few species wait 20 or 30 years before flowering and then die. Other species flower at odd intervals for many years. One species flowered at 14,39 and then 7 year intervals. All bamboos of the same species flower at the same time even if they are taken to the other side of the world. How do bamboos count the years? People have suggested that sunspots may be involved but no one really knows.

Record breakers

The amazing Welwitschia

The *Welwitschia mirabilis* plant only ever grows two leaves although it may live for 100 years or more. The leaves grow about 5-8 centimetres a year and the largest recorded leaves were 8.2 metres by 2 metres.

Largest leaves

The Raffia Palm has the largest leaves in the world. Its leaves measure up to twenty metres in length and are taller than most trees.

Smallest flowering plant

A floating duckweed called *Wolffia arrhiza* is the smallest flowering plant in the world. Its fronds are only 0.5 – 1.2 millimetres across and 25 of these plants would fit across your fingernail.

Deepest roots

The deepest roots ever reported were those of a wild fig tree in South Africa, which grew to a depth of 120 metres.

Largest living thing

The largest living thing on earth is a Giant Sequoia Tree from California, U.S.A., which is called "General Sherman". It is 83 metres tall and measures 24.11 metres round the trunk. It contains enough timber for forty bungalows or 5,000,000,000 matches.

First space plant

The first plant to flower and produce seeds in the zero gravity of space is called Arabidopsis. It has a short life cycle of about forty days and was grown on board the Soviet Union's Salyut-7 space station in 1982.

Largest water plant

The Giant Water Lily from the Amazon is the world's largest water plant. Its leaves can grow up to two metres across and they are strong enough to take the weight of a child. Thick ribs under the leaf help it to float.

Largest rose tree

A "Lady Banks" rose tree at Tombstone, Arizona, U.S.A. has a trunk 101 centimetres thick, stands 2.74 metres high and covers an area of 499 square metres. It is supported by 68 posts and 150 people can sit underneath it.

World's oldest living thing

A lichen from Antarctica is thought to be at least 10,000 years old and could be much older. Other lichens in Alaska are at least 9,000 years old and grow only 3.4mm in a hundred years.

World's oldest seed plant

The ancestors of the Gingko or Maidenhair Tree first appeared in China about 180,000,000 years ago. This was the Jurassic Period, when dinosaurs roamed the earth. The Gingko trees alive today look very much like their ancestors from these ancient times.

Slowest flowering plant

The rare *Puya raimondii* from the Andes does not flower until it is about 150 years old. After this the plant dies.

Most and least nutritious fruit

The **most** nutritious fruit in the world is the Avocado. It contains 741 calories per edible pound. The **least** nutritious fruit in the world is the cucumber. It contains only 73 calories per edible pound.

Hardiest seeds

Arctic Lupin seeds found frozen in the soil in the Canadian Yukon were believed to be between 10,000 and 15,000 years old. Some of them sprouted and grew into plants; one even developed flowers.

Monster fruit and vegetables

Here are just some of the largest fruit and vegetables ever recorded.
Cabbage...51.8 kg
Cauliflower...23.9 kg
Tomato...1.9 kg
Pumpkin...171.4 kg
Mushroom...190 cm (round the edge of the cap)
Lemon...2.65 kg
Pineapple...7.5 kg
Melon...40.8 kg

31

Were they true or false?

page 5. Lianas grow as tall as the Eiffel Tower and are strong enough to take the weight of an elephant.
Possibly true. The Eiffel Tower is 320 metres high and there are a few lianas on record with stems over 300 metres long. A tangle of liana stems can hold up a giant jungle tree so several lianas together **might** be able to take the weight of an elephant (about 5.7 tonnes).

page 7. Green potatoes can poison children.
True. Green potatoes contain large amounts of strong poisons called solanines, which are especially dangerous to children. The poisons are not destroyed by boiling or cooking.

page 9. Ants make apples grow on Oak Trees.
False. A structure called an oak apple gall does grow on some Oak Trees but a female **wasp** causes the tree to grow the "apple" by laying her eggs in an Oak bud.

page 12. Blue roses flower only in China.
False. There is, as yet, no such thing as a true blue rose — or a black rose.

page 15. Flowers make perfume for bees.
Partly true. A species of Euglossa bee from Latin America collects scent from orchids. The scent attracts other male bees and the sight of a glittering group of male bees in turn attracts female bees.

page 17. Orchids are used to make ice cream.
Partly true. The flavouring in some kinds of vanilla ice cream comes from the cured seed pod of an orchid called *Vanilla planifolia*.

page 19. Mexican beans jump away from their parent plant.
False. A caterpillar living inside the beans of the Mexican Arrow Plant makes them leap into the air.

page 20. Fungi are strong enough to grow through roads and pavements.
True. Fungi such as the Ink Cap can break up asphalt and even lift paving stones.

page 23. Clubmosses are used to make fireworks.
True. The spore cases of the Stag's Horn Clubmoss produce a bright yellow powder, which was used at one time to make fireworks.

page 25. Flowers grow at the top of Mount Everest.
False. Everest is 8,848 metres high and the highest altitude at which any flowering plant has been found is 6,135 metres. This was for a plant called *Stellaria decumbens* in the Himalayas.

page 27. Plants scream when they are thirsty.
Partly true. An Australian scientist found that plants make clicking noises when they are thirsty. The noises are caused by the vibrations of the tiny water pipes inside plants.

---

page 6. How many pebble plants?

There are **10** different kinds of pebble plant in the picture.

Index